PRENTICE HALL

UNITED STATES HISTORY

All-in-One
Teaching Resources

The New Deal
(1932–1941)

PEARSON
Prentice
Hall

Upper Saddle River, New Jersey
Boston, Massachusetts

Acknowledgements

Page 23: ROLL ON, COLUMBIA. Words by Woody Guthrie. Music based on GOODNIGHT, IRENE by Huddie Ledbetter and John A. Lomaz. TRO-Copyright © 1936 (Renewed) 1957 (Renewed) and 1963 (Renewed). Ludlow Music, Inc., New York, NY. Used by permission.

NOTE: Every effort has been made to locate the copyright owner of material reprinted in this book. Omissions brought to our attention will be corrected in subsequent editions.

Upper Saddle River, New Jersey
Boston, Massachusetts

ISBN 0-13-203686-X

1 2 3 4 5 6 7 8 9 10   10 09 08 07 06

* The Issues Connector worksheet may be modified for students as follows:
   L1 Ask students to read one of the excerpts. Review any vocabulary that may cause difficulty in comprehension. Then, have students rewrite the excerpt in their own words. During class discussion, call on these students first to share their work.
   L2 Have students read one of the excerpts and the corresponding background note. Have them identify any difficult vocabulary, and review definitions with them. Then, have students summarize the selection in a short paragraph and explain the context in which it was written.
   L3 Give students the background notes and primary sources. Have them complete the worksheet.
   L4 Give students the background notes and primary sources. Have them complete the worksheet. As an extension, ask students to conduct a debate based on the question asked on the feature in the textbook. As an alternate activity, have students find current events articles that relate to the issue involved. Ask them to compare the articles to the excerpts given and explain their own position on the issue.

Name _____ Class _____ Date _____

Letter Home

Dear Family:

Over the coming weeks, our United States history class will be reading a chapter called The New Deal. The following information will give you some background to the content your student will be studying.

By the presidential election of 1932, Americans had endured three years of economic hardship during the Great Depression. President Hoover's failed relief policies were replaced in 1932 by the new ideas of Franklin Delano Roosevelt. Hoover adopted a policy of minimal government intervention to provide relief during the depression, but Roosevelt replaced this approach with his New Deal, a policy that would establish various government programs to provide economic relief for Americans. During the first hundred days of his administration, Roosevelt established programs to stabilize banks, modernize regions of the country by providing electricity, and stimulate industries in order to provide jobs for workers. Although Roosevelt's programs provided much needed relief, some people opposed the government's expanding involvement in the economy and in the lives of Americans. Also, many argued that Roosevelt's programs had not done enough to help Americans find relief from the Depression. Throughout the rest of the 1930s, Roosevelt worked to improve economic conditions for struggling Americans. Although some of his programs still exist, debate continues as to whether the increased government involvement has been a positive change for the United States.

While Roosevelt was facing criticism for the New Deal, the country experienced changes on many levels. Women played a prominent role during the New Deal, as evidenced by the work of First Lady Eleanor Roosevelt. African Americans saw some advances as President Roosevelt established what was know as the Black Cabinet to advise him on issues that affected African Americans. Native Americans achieved greater control over their lands as a result of the Indian Reorganization Act. New political alliances emerged as the Democratic Party unified African Americans, Southern whites, and blue-collar workers, all of whom benefited from New Deal programs. The Great Depression also greatly affected American culture as films and radio fostered a sense of escapism to give Americans relief from the depressed economic environment.

In the weeks ahead, your student may wish to share what he or she is learning with you. Please participate in your child's educational experience through discussion and involvement.

Sincerely,

EL NUEVO TRATO
Carta para el hogar

Estimada familia,

En las próximas semanas, nuestra clase de historia de Estados Unidos va a leer un capítulo llamado "El Nuevo Trato". La siguiente información le dará a usted algunos conocimientos sobre el tema que su estudiante va a estudiar.

Para la elección presidencial de 1932, los estadounidenses habían soportado tres años de dificultades económicas durante la Gran Depresión. Las políticas de alivio del presidente Hoover fracasaron y fueron reemplazadas en 1932 por una nueva visión de Franklin Delano Roosevelt. Hoover había adoptado una política de mínima intervención gubernamental para ofrecer alivio durante la Depresión, pero Roosevelt reemplazó este enfoque con su Nueva Trato, una política que establecería varios programas gubernamentales para ofrecer alivio económico a los estadounidenses. Durante los primeros cien días de su administración, Roosevelt estableció programas para estabilizar los bancos, modernizar regiones del país proporcionando electricidad, y estimular las industrias para crear empleos para los trabajadores. Aunque los programas de Roosevelt proporcionaron un alivio muy necesario, algunas personas se oponían a la creciente participación del gobierno en la economía y en la vida de los estadounidenses. También, muchos argumentaban que los programas de Roosevelt no habían hecho lo suficiente para ayudar a los estadounidenses a hallar alivio de la Depresión. Durante el resto de la década de 1930, Roosevelt trabajó para mejorar las condiciones económicas de los estadounidenses con problemas. Aunque algunos de sus programas todavía existen, el debate continúa sobre si la mayor participación del gobierno ha sido un cambio positivo para Estados Unidos.

Mientras Roosevelt enfrentaba críticas por el Nuevo Trato, el país experimentaba cambios a muchos niveles. Las mujeres jugaron un papel predominante durante el Nuevo Trato, como se evidencia en el trabajo de la primera dama Eleanor Roosevelt. Los africano-americanos vieron avances ya que el presidente Roosevelt estableció lo que se conoció como el Gabinete Negro, para que le aconsejara sobre los problemas que enfrentaban los africano-americanos. Los indígenas americanos lograron un mayor control sobre sus tierras como resultado de la Ley de Reorganización Indígena. Emergieron nuevas alianzas a medida que el partido Demócrata unificó a los trabajadores africano-americanos, sureños blancos y obreros, todos los cuales se beneficiaron de los programas del Nuevo Trato. La Gran Depresión también afectó en gran medida a la cultura estadounidense, y las películas y la radio ofrecían una sensación de escape para dar alivio a los estadounidenses del ambiente de depresión económica.

En las próximas semanas, es posible que su estudiante quiera compartir con usted lo que ha aprendido. Por favor participe en la experiencia educativa de su hijo o hija a través de conversaciones e involucrándose en su trabajo.

Atentamente,

THE NEW DEAL 1932–1941

1. FDR Offers Relief and Recovery

Pacing
2 periods
1 block

L1	Special Needs
L2	Basic to Average
L3	All Students
L4	Average to Advanced

Section Objectives

- Analyze the impact Franklin D. Roosevelt had on the American people after becoming President.
- Describe the programs that were part of the first New Deal and their immediate impact.
- Identify critical responses to the New Deal.

Terms and People • Franklin D. Roosevelt • Eleanor Roosevelt • New Deal • fireside chat • FDIC • TVA • CCC • NRA • PWA • Charles Coughlin • Huey Long

Focus Question: How did the New Deal attempt to address the problems of the depression?

PREPARE TO READ

Build Background Knowledge
Preview the section and remind students that the United States was in a depression at the beginning of Roosevelt's presidency.

Set a Purpose
Have students discuss the Witness History Selection. Point out the Section Focus Question, and have students fill in the Note Taking graphic organizer.

Preview Key Terms
Preview the section's Key Terms.

Instructional Resources
❑ **WITNESS HISTORY** Audio CD

❑ **All in One Teaching Resources**
   L3 Preread the Chapter, p. 8
   L3 Analyze Visuals, p. 10
   L3 Vocabulary Builder, p. 11
   L3 Reading Strategy, p. 12

❑ **Reading and Note Taking Study Guide**
   (On-Level, Adapted, and Spanish)
   Section 1

TEACH

Roosevelt Takes Charge
Explain Roosevelt's background and rise to the presidency.

The First Hundred Days Provide Instant Action
Discuss the First New Deal's policies for relief, reform, and recovery.

Opposition to the New Deal Emerges
Examine why people opposed Roosevelt's New Deal.

Instructional Resources
❑ **All in One Teaching Resources**
   L1 L2 Interpreting a Political Cartoon: The New Deal, p. 19
   L3 Interpreting a Political Cartoon: FDR and the New Deal, p. 20

❑ **Color Transparencies**
   L3 Civilian Conservation Corps

❑ **Note Taking Transparencies,** B-107

ASSESS/RETEACH

Assess Progress
Evaluate student comprehension with the Section Assessment and Section Quiz.

Reteach
Assign the Reading and Note Taking Study Guide to help struggling students.

Extend
Have students read and complete the Enrichment worksheet, *Debate: The New Deal.*

Instructional Resources
❑ **All in One Teaching Resources**
   L4 Enrichment: Debate: The New Deal, p. 13
   L3 Section Quiz, p. 24

❑ **Reading and Note Taking Study Guide**
❑ **Progress Monitoring Transparencies,** 103

Audio support is available for this section.
Modify lesson with notes found on the bottom of the Teacher's Edition.

THE NEW DEAL 1932–1941

2. The Second New Deal

Pacing
2 periods
1 block

L1	Special Needs
L2	Basic to Average
L3	All Students
L4	Average to Advanced

Section Objectives

■ Discuss the programs of social and economic reform in the second New Deal.

■ Explain how New Deal legislation affected the growth of organized labor.

■ Describe the impact of Roosevelt's court-packing plan on the course of the New Deal.

Terms and People • second New Deal • WPA • John Maynard Keynes • pump priming • Social Security Act • Wagner Act • collective bargaining • Fair Labor Standards Act • CIO • sit-down strikes • court packing

Focus Question: What major issues did the second New Deal address?

PREPARE TO READ

Build Background Knowledge
Preview the section and remind students that opposition to the New Deal existed from the beginning of Roosevelt's presidency.

Set a Purpose
Have students discuss the Witness History Selection. Point out the Section Focus Question, and have students fill in the Note Taking graphic organizer.

Preview Key Terms
Preview the section's Key Terms.

Instructional Resources
❑ **WITNESS HISTORY** Audio CD

❑ **All in One Teaching Resources**
❑ **Reading and Note Taking Study Guide**
   (On-Level, Adapted, and Spanish)
   Section 2

TEACH

Extending Social and Economic Reform
Discuss how the second New Deal affected the unemployed, the elderly, and farmers.

Labor Unions Find a New Energy
Explore how labor unions gained rights for workers.

Challenges to the New Deal
Explain the Supreme Court's opposition to the New Deal and the economic downturns.

Instructional Resources

❑ **All in One Teaching Resources**
   L3 Reading a Chart: New Deal Programs, p. 21
❑ **Skills Handbook**
   L3 Analyze Graphic Data, p. 26
❑ **Color Transparencies**
   L3 Critics of the New Deal
❑ **Note Taking Transparencies,** B-108

ASSESS/RETEACH

Assess Progress
Evaluate student comprehension with the Section Assessment and Section Quiz.

Reteach
Assign the Reading and Note Taking Study Guide to help struggling students.

Extend
Have students write newspaper headlines about the New Deal.

Instructional Resources

❑ **All in One Teaching Resources**
   L3 Section Quiz, p. 25
❑ **Reading and Note Taking Study Guide**
❑ **Progress Monitoring Transparencies,** 104

THE NEW DEAL 1932–1941

3. Effects of the New Deal

Pacing
2 periods
1 block

L1 Special Needs
L2 Basic to Average
L3 All Students
L4 Average to Advanced

Section Objectives

■ Describe how the New Deal affected different groups in American society.

■ Analyze how the New Deal changed the shape of American party politics.

■ Discuss the impact of Franklin D. Roosevelt on the presidency.

Terms and People • Black Cabinet • Mary McLeod Bethune • Indian New Deal • New Deal coalition • welfare state

Focus Question: How did the New Deal change the social, economic, and political landscape of the United States for future generations?

PREPARE TO READ

Build Background Knowledge
Preview the section and inform students that Roosevelt was elected President four times.

Set a Purpose
Have students discuss the Witness History Selection. Point out the Section Focus Question, and have students fill in the Note Taking graphic organizer.

Preview Key Terms
Preview the section's Key Terms.

Instructional Resources
❑ **WITNESS HISTORY** Audio CD

❑ **All in One** **Teaching Resources**
❑ **Reading and Note Taking Study Guide**
(On-Level, Adapted, and Spanish)
Section 3

TEACH

Women Help Lead the New Deal
Discuss in what ways Eleanor Roosevelt changed the role of First Lady.

African Americans Make Advances and Face Challenges
Discuss the Black Cabinet.

The New Deal Affects Native Americans
Explain the Indian Reorganization Act.

The New Deal Creates a New Political Coalition
Explain how the New Deal changed politics.

The Role of Government Expands
Discuss the New Deal and the role of government.

Instructional Resources

❑ **All in One** **Teaching Resources**
L3 Issues Connector: Government's Role in the Economy, p. 15
L3 Biography: Eleanor Roosevelt, p. 22
❑ **Color Transparencies**
L3 The New Deal
❑ **Note Taking Transparencies,** B-109

ASSESS/RETEACH

Assess Progress
Evaluate student comprehension with the Section Assessment and Section Quiz.

Reteach
Assign the Reading and Note Taking Study Guide to help struggling students.

Extend
Have students write an essay for or against the statement: FDR's New Deal preserved the United States as a democratic society.

Instructional Resources

❑ **All in One** **Teaching Resources**
L3 Section Quiz, p. 26
❑ **Reading and Note Taking Study Guide**
❑ **Progress Monitoring Transparencies,** 105

THE NEW DEAL 1932–1941

4. Culture of the 1930s

Pacing
1.5 periods
.75 block

L1	Special Needs
L2	Basic to Average
L3	All Students
L4	Average to Advanced

Section Objectives

- Trace the growth of radio and the movies in the 1930s and the changes in popular culture.
- Describe the major themes of literature of the New Deal era.

Terms and People • *The Wizard of Oz* • Frank Capra • *War of the Worlds* • Federal Art Project • mural • Dorthea Lange • John Steinbeck • Lillian Hellman

Focus Question: How did the men and women of the depression find relief from their hardships in the popular culture?

PREPARE TO READ

Build Background Knowledge
Preview the chapter and discuss movies and comic books from the 1930s.

Set a Purpose
Have students discuss the Witness History Selection. Point out the Section Focus Question, and have students fill in the Note Taking graphic organizer.

Preview Key Terms
Preview the section's Key Terms.

Instructional Resources
- ❑ **WITNESS HISTORY** Audio CD
- ❑ All in One **Teaching Resources**
- ❑ **Reading and Note Taking Study Guide** (On-Level, Adapted, and Spanish) Section 4

TEACH

Movies and Radio Captivate Americans
Explain how people turned to entertainment to relieve the effects of the depression.

The New Deal and the Arts
Discuss the New Deal's impact on the arts.

The Literature of the Depression
Discuss the rise of working class heroes.

Instructional Resources
- ❑ All in One **Teaching Resources**
  - **L3** Link to Literature: "ROLL ON, COLUMBIA," p. 23
- ❑ **Color Transparencies**
  - **L3** Big Bands Swing
- ❑ **Note Taking Transparencies,** B-110

ASSESS/RETEACH

Assess Progress
Evaluate student comprehension with the Section Assessment and Section Quiz.

Reteach
Assign the Reading and Note Taking Study Guide to help struggling students.

Extend
Extend the lesson by having students complete the online activity on producing a multimedia presentation.

Instructional Resources
- ❑ All in One **Teaching Resources**
  - **L3** Section Quiz, p. 27
  - **L1** **L2** Chapter Test A, p. 28
  - **L3** Chapter Test B, p. 31
- ❑ **Reading and Note Taking Study Guide**
- ❑ **Progress Monitoring Transparencies,** 106

Name _____ Class _____ Date _____

Preread the Chapter: Why and How?

What is **Prereading?** It is a reading comprehension strategy. This graphic organizer aids you in prereading this chapter.

Checklist: *Place a check on the line when you have completed the following:*

_____ Read all items in the Chapter Opener.

_____ Read the titles of the charts, graphs, maps, and timeline in the Quick Study Guide and Concept Connector Cumulative Review.

_____ Read the chapter assessment.

Before you read each section of your text, look at the following material. (Chapters may have 3, 4, or 5 sections.) Check the sections as you complete the review.

Sections: 1_____ 2_____ 3_____ 4_____ 5_____ Read the Focus Question, the section opener information in the side column, and each boldface heading and subheading.

Sections: 1_____ 2_____ 3_____ 4_____ 5_____ Looked over all words that are underlined or in boldface type.

Sections: 1_____ 2_____ 3_____ 4_____ 5_____ Read all review questions within the section.

Complete the following:

1. Chapter title: _____

2. Write the main idea of each section based on its Focus Question.

   Section 1: _____
   _____

   Section 2: _____
   _____

   Section 3: _____
   _____

   Section 4: _____
   _____

   Section 5: _____
   _____

Preread the Chapter: Why and How? (Continued)

3. List three visual aids included in the chapter (e.g., pictures, maps, charts, diagrams, features). Describe how they will aid your understanding of the chapter.

(1) _____

_____

(2) _____

_____

(3) _____

_____

4. Describe one new or important idea you learned from reading the Quick Study Guide.

_____

_____

5. Identify two unfamiliar words that you noticed during your prereading, and determine from the context what you think the new word means.

Word #1 _____ Part of Speech _____

Clues to meaning _____

Predicted meaning _____

Word #2 _____ Part of Speech _____

Clues to meaning _____

Predicted meaning _____

6. After previewing this chapter, were you able to understand what the chapter is about?

Not understood _____ Somewhat understood _____ Easily understood _____

7. Copy the heading (titles in blue print) that you predict will be the most difficult to understand.

_____

_____

8. How many pages are in the chapter? _____

9. Estimate the time it will take you to read the chapter. _____

Analyze Visuals

Images are an effective way to communicate information. There are many types of visuals, such as photographs, paintings, and Infographics. Visuals tell a story in a dramatic or vivid style. Just as with any primary or secondary source, it is important to look closely and ask questions to determine the meaning and reliability of the visual.

Use this outline to help you better understand ideas or events conveyed by a visual. Answer these questions to the best of your ability.

Title of visual Page

1. What is the topic of the visual (what is happening)?

_____

2. Focus on the details and list three that you find in the visual. How does each help convey information about the topic?

_____

_____

_____

3. Assume you are one of the individuals in the picture, or that you were present when the image was made.

   (a) Describe who you are.

   _____

   (b) Explain what your reaction might have been to the situation.

   _____

   _____

4. The creator often reveals a bias about the subject or an attempt to get a response from the viewer. Is there anything you see in the image that tells the creator's point of view?

_____

_____

5. Write your own caption for the image.

_____

Name _____ Class _____ Date _____

Vocabulary Builder

Think of Memory Clues

To learn new vocabulary, you may find it helpful to think of **memory clues.** Memory clues can be pictures, words, phrases, and names that remind you of a word's meaning. Perhaps a certain person or place helps you connect meaning to a word. The example below provides visual and verbal memory clues for the word *ensure.*

Example

Word	Definition	Memory Clues
ensure	to make safe, guarantee	minimum wage, provide employment

Sentence The New Deal helped <u>ensure</u> jobs and minimum wages.

Directions: *Review the words listed below in your textbook. Then, on another piece of paper, complete the table by recording the definition, providing one or two memory clues, and writing a sentence for each word. Remember that your clues can be pictures or words and phrases.*

1. Word	Definition	Memory Clues
gender		
Sentence		
2. Word	Definition	Memory Clues
ethnic		
Sentence		

THE NEW DEAL

Reading Strategy

Connect Ideas

When you read, your main goal is to get meaning from the words on the page. The best way to achieve this goal is to connect the text you are reading with information that you already know.

A KWL chart can help you connect your previous knowledge with new information. The K stands for what you already know, the W for what you want to discover, and the L for what you learned after completing the reading. Read the following paragraph on New Deal programs and the sample KWL chart.

> Roosevelt was convinced that the federal government needed to play an active role in promoting recovery and providing relief to Americans. A number of his New Deal programs sought to reform the nation's financial institutions. One act created the Federal Deposit Insurance Corporation, which insured bank deposits up to $5,000. Other of Roosevelt's New Deal programs aimed at easing the desperate plight of American farmers. Congress passed the Agricultural Adjustment Act to end overproduction and raise crop prices.

Know	Want to Know	Learned
Roosevelt's New Deal programs tried to combat the depression.	How did the New Deal aid farmers?	The Agricultural Adjustment Act was passed to end overproduction and raise crop prices.

Directions: *On a separate sheet of paper, make a KWL chart like the one shown below. Reread Section 1 under the heading "Opposition to the New Deal Emerges." Before reading the paragraphs, read the title and fill in the Know column and the Want to Know column. Then when you are finished reading, fill in the Learned column with any new facts you learned while reading. Use your chart to answer the questions below. Write your answers below your chart.*

> **Hint:** Look at the question you wrote in the Want to Know column. Look for the answer to that question in the paragraphs.

Know	Want to Know	Learned

1. What is the main focus of these paragraphs?

2. What new information did you learn from the paragraphs?

3. Using the information you learned as prior information, what is another question you could ask about this topic?

THE NEW DEAL

Enrichment: Debate

The New Deal

President Roosevelt changed the role of the federal government by placing more responsibility for economic recovery on the federal government. One New Deal program, the Civilian Conservation Corps, gave millions of unemployed Americans jobs repairing the nation's soil, conserving water, and preserving natural resources. Today, with pollution problems and unemployment still concerns, what if the government reinstated the CCC?

Your assignment: Research the benefits and problems associated with the Civilian Conservation Corps. Use the information you gather to plan and present a debate on the following topic: Should the federal government today reinstate this New Deal program?

Suggested materials: Dry-erase board and markers (to detail key points in the debate) or poster board; note cards (to remember key points while debating), map of the United States (showing conservation areas), graphs or charts illustrating unemployment levels

Suggested procedures:

1. As a group, decide who will take each side of the issue and who will judge the debate. Will the teacher, a panel of judges, or the audience judge?

2. Determine the rules for the debate—speaking order, time limits, and so on.

3. Research what conservation meant in the United States in the 1930s. Then, determine how the CCC was designed to help unemployed Americans, and research the program's benefits and problems. How would the new CCC achieve the same benefits and avoid the same problems?

4. Research unemployment problems today as well as conservation issues. Why would some people oppose the new CCC? Why would others support it? Read the questions on the following page for research ideas.

5. Support your arguments. Begin by identifying evidence that will support your side of the issue. Identify evidence that you can use to disprove arguments that you think your opponents will be most likely to use.

6. Organize your thoughts in an outline. Arrange the arguments and the evidence you will need to prove or disprove your position.

7. Anticipate your opponent's arguments, and prepare rebuttals for his or her key positions.

8. Prepare for your presentation by putting your arguments, evidence, and rebuttals on note cards. Read your note cards over several times to become familiar with them.

9. After your debate, use the chart on the next page to recall the debate's important points before making your final decision on the new CCC.

Name _____ Class _____ Date _____

Enrichment: Debate

The New Deal

Directions: *Consider the following questions as you research your side of the debate.*

1. What areas of the country would benefit from the new CCC?

2. Who would be eligible to work for the new CCC? How long would someone be able to work for the CCC?

3. Who would oversee the new CCC?

4. What other programs already exist that are similar to the new CCC? Would the new CCC be part of those programs or take their place?

5. What would the application process include for people who want to work for the new CCC?

6. Where would workers in the new CCC live while working on sites away from their homes?

7. Would education be offered to the recruits of the new CCC? If so, for how long? Who will give the training? In what areas? What if someone were to not do well or not want the education?

8. How would the government pay for the new CCC?

You should base your answers to these questions on factual information. However, you should also use your creativity to eliminate problems and address concerns.

Directions: *Use the following chart to record important points made during the debate. When the debate is over, use the information you recorded to make your final decision.*

New CCC Benefits	New CCC Benefits Rebuttals	New CCC Problems	New CCC Problems Rebuttals

THE NEW DEAL

Issues Connector: Government's Role in the Economy

Since the U.S. federal government was created, its role and functions have undergone revision. Although some politicians strive for a larger government that plays a more active role in American life, others fight to keep government small and curtail its functions and responsibilities. Government's role in the economy has been an especially important area of debate.

U.S. Constitution: The U.S. Constitution includes guidelines for the federal government's role in the economy of the United States. However, some of the Constitution's language is vague, allowing lawmakers room to create laws in reaction to new economic situations.

Tariff of 1816: The War of 1812 between the United States and England caused England to refuse to trade with the United States. People in the United States had to begin manufacturing goods they had previously imported. At the end of the war, U.S. leaders wanted to protect new manufacturing business from cheap European imports of iron and textiles and so they created the Tariff of 1816. The tariff placed a 25 percent tax on goods from Europe. Europeans raised the prices of their goods in the United States to pay for the new tariff. Southern states, who relied on imports because of their agrarian economies, resented a tariff that they saw as a tax on them to support Northern manufacturers.

Sherman Antitrust Act, 1890: The late 1800s was a time of trusts, or anti-competition agreements. These agreements meant that companies agreed to control prices, buy out competitors, force unwanted goods on customers, and limit competition, so some state legislatures passed laws to curb trusts. However, these laws only controlled trade within states. Public pressure forced the federal government to pass the Sherman Antitrust Act, which made all monopolies and trusts illegal. However, the act's language was vague and difficult to enforce. Further legislation built upon the act, which was an important step in government regulation of business. Recently, the government filed suits against companies such as Microsoft for violations of laws built on the Sherman Antitrust Act.

Agricultural Adjustment Act, 1933: Franklin D. Roosevelt saw the Great Depression as a time when the government needed to take control of the economy. During his first 100 days in office, FDR and the Congress passed 15 bills known as the First New Deal. The Agricultural Adjustment Act paid farmers not to grow crops, so that prices would rise again, and farmers would find relief. Under the act, surplus food was also sent to needy families and to schools for use in lunches. Later, this act was amended to give Presidents the power to regulate imported foods because they could interfere with the sales of American-grown food in the United States.

THE NEW DEAL

Issues Connector: Government's Role in the Economy

Tax Cuts, 2001 and 2006: The downfall of many social programs, such as New Deal programs, was that these programs led to a larger government with a greater role in people's lives. To combat the rising costs of government spending, some Presidents after Roosevelt have implemented tax cuts. President George W. Bush signed a bill in 2001 that implemented controversial tax cuts. While the Bush administration said that many Americans benefited from these cuts, some people criticized the bill for benefiting only high-income households. However, Bush signed another bill in 2006 that extended his tax cuts. His goal was to stimulate the economy not through government intervention, like FDR did, but by letting people decide how to spend their own money.

Name _____ Class _____ Date _____

Issues Connector: Government's Role in the Economy

Section 8. The Congress shall have power to lay and collect taxes, . . . to pay the debts and provide for the common defense and general welfare of the United States . . . To borrow money on the credit of the United States . . . To regulate commerce with foreign nations, and among the several states....

—*United States Constitution, Article 1, Section 8*

"Sir, I am convinced that it would be impolitic, as well as unjust, to aggravate the burdens of the people for the purpose of favoring the manufacturers; . . . The agricultures bear the whole brunt of the war [of 1812] and taxation, and remain poor, while the others run in the ring of pleasure, and fatten upon them."

—*John Randolph, on the Protective Tariff of 1816*

"Economic growth begins with the hard work of the American people and good policies in Washington, D.C. . . . . [W]e delivered the largest tax relief since Ronald Reagan was in the White House. . . . The American people have used their money better than the government ever could have. They've used the tax relief to provide for their families and create jobs and help American economy become the envy of the industrialized world"

—*George W. Bush, May, 2006*

"**Sec. 1.** Every contract, combination in the form of trust or other- wise, or conspiracy, in restraint of trade or commerce among the several States . . . is hereby declared to be illegal.

Sec. 7. Any person who shall be injured in his business or property by any other person or corporation by reason of anything forbidden or declared to be unlawful by this act, may sue . . . ."

—*Sherman Antitrust Act, 1890*

Government's Role in the Economy

"An Act to relieve the existing national economic emergency by increasing agricultural purchasing power. . . .

Sec. 2 (1) To establish and maintain such balance between production and consumption of agricultural commodities . . .

Sec. 2 (3) To protect the consumers' interest by readjusting farm production. . . ."

—*Agricultural Adjustment Act, 1933*

THE NEW DEAL

Issues Connector: Government's Role in the Economy

Directions: *Read the excerpts regarding the government's role in the economy. Then answer the questions that follow.*

1. What trend does the timeline show for government involvement in the economy?

   _____

   _____

2. What powers does the Sherman Antitrust Act give to consumers?

   _____

   _____

3. How do you think Randolph would feel about the government passing the Agriculture Adjustment Act to subsidize farmers?

   _____

   _____

4. What reason does President Bush give for believing that the government should encourage self-government in its citizens?

   _____

   _____

5. **Draw Conclusions** How might FDR have argued that his Agricultural Adjustment Act was constitutional?

   _____

   _____

   _____

6. **Link Past and Present** What type of President would you most likely vote for, one who promotes government control of the economy, or one who opposes government intervention? Explain your answer.

   _____

   _____

   _____

   _____

THE NEW DEAL

Interpreting a Political Cartoon

The New Deal was a controversial plan to help the United States survive the Great Depression. Many people thought the U.S. government had not done enough to help people in the past. When Roosevelt took office, he enacted many programs designed to help Americans. Some people supported these programs, and others did not. ◆ *Use the political cartoon below to answer the questions that follow on a separate sheet of paper.*

The New Deal

Dr. New Deal, Getty Images Inc./Hulton Archive Photos

Questions to Think About

1. What do the bottles on the table represent?

2. How does this cartoonist show Congressional support for New Deal programs?

3. Make Inferences Does this cartoonist support New Deal programs? Explain your answer.

THE NEW DEAL

Interpreting a Political Cartoon

Roosevelt called his controversial plan to help the United States survive the Great Depression the New Deal. Many people looked to Roosevelt to stop the poverty and unemployment that characterized the depression. Others thought that the government should allow businesses and people to help themselves rather than become involved in stopping the economic crisis. ◆ *Use the political cartoon below to answer the questions that follow on a separate sheet of paper.*

FDR and the New Deal

"Looks as if the new leadership was really going to lead". The Granger Collection, New York

Questions to Think About

1. What is Roosevelt doing in the cartoon?

2. What relationship between FDR and Congress does this cartoon show?

3. Detect Bias What does this cartoonist probably think about FDR's leadership?

Name _____ Class _____ Date _____

Reading a Chart

Roosevelt's New Deal created many new programs and responsibilities for the government. Some of his programs gave money directly to people, and others provided jobs. These programs cost millions of dollars, and some of the benefits and issues they created are still apparent in the United States today. ◆ *Use the information in the chart below as well as in the chart "The Second New Deal" in section 2 in your textbook to answer the questions that follow on a separate sheet of paper.*

New Deal Programs

Program	Year Ended	Total Amount Spent
Works Progress Administration (WPA)	1943	about $11 billion
National Youth Administration (NYA)	1943	over $4.6 million
United States Housing Authority (USHA)	1939	about $540 million
Public Works Administration (PWA)	1941	over $6 billion
Civilian Conservation Corps (CCC)	1942	about $3.5 billion

Questions to Think About

1. Why do you think FDR's New Deal programs were often referred to as "alphabet soup"?

2. Which programs listed in the chart and in the book were specifically aimed to help lower the unemployment rate?

3. **Draw Inferences** Why might some people have argued that government was becoming too big because of the New Deal?

4. **Draw Conclusions** What do you think Roosevelt saw as the government's responsibility during the depression?

Biography

Eleanor Roosevelt led a life of public service, and her impact on the position of First Lady is still felt today. ◆ *As you read, think about how Eleanor Roosevelt changed the expectations of the First Lady's role and the way she changed how the nation helped the poor and minorities. Then, on a separate sheet of paper, answer the questions that follow.*

Eleanor Roosevelt (1884–1962)

Born in 1884, Eleanor Roosevelt lived through many changes in the United States and the world. When her husband, Franklin Delano Roosevelt, became President of the United States in 1933, Eleanor Roosevelt was determined "to do things on my own, to use my own mind and abilities for my own aims." She had visions that she wanted to see put into motion and struggled to balance that and her role as First Lady.

Eleanor Roosevelt, ©White House Collection, Courtesy White House Historical Association

When Eleanor Roosevelt first entered the White House, she did not push her own programs, but strove to improve on her husband's New Deal programs. One of her goals was to see women play a larger role in Washington politics. She held weekly meetings with female reporters and pushed for women to hold political office in the White House. Her efforts led to women joining the NRA Labor Advisory Board as well as NRA Consumer Advisory Board. After noticing that two of her husband's plans ignored unemployed women, she lobbied to have women's divisions created in these plans with women to lead them.

Eleanor Roosevelt believed that there could be no real democracy if racism continued as part of American culture.

She was the first white resident of Washington, D.C. to become a member of the local chapters of the NAACP and the National Urban League. In FDR's second term, she served as co-chair of the committee to abolish the poll tax. She supported National Sharecroppers Week, and pushed the AAA to acknowledge that their policies discriminated against African American farmers.

Eleanor Roosevelt also wanted to improve the lives of the poor. She worked with the Secretary of the Interior to improve conditions in a West Virginia coal town. The First Lady visited the new community, Arthurdale, and even danced with miners. During World War II, Eleanor Roosevelt extended her passion for helping the poor to European refugees. She lobbied Congress to bend the Immigration laws to allow refugees fleeing persecution in Europe to enter the United States.

Even after leaving the White House, Eleanor Roosevelt continued to change the world. She used her mind to follow her aims and spent her time fighting for racial justice, world peace, and women's rights until her death in 1962.

Questions to Think About

1. What three causes did Eleanor Roosevelt fight to support when she was First Lady?

2. How did Eleanor Roosevelt take her fight to help the poor outside the borders of the United States?

3. **Draw Inferences** What obstacles did Eleanor Roosevelt have to overcome to put her agenda to work?

4. **Link Past and Present** What would the First Lady today think of Eleanor Roosevelt?

THE NEW DEAL

Link to Literature

One particular New Deal public works project had a long-lasting effect on the American West. The Bonneville Dam in the Pacific Northwest helped control flooding and provided hydroelectric power to citizens when private companies could not. In 1941, the U.S. Department of the Interior hired Woody Guthrie to write songs about the Columbia River and the dams being built there. This song was adopted as the state folk song of Washington state in 1987. ◆ *As you read, think about what life was like in America during this time and what experiences Guthrie may have endured during the Great Depression and Dust Bowl. Then, on a separate sheet of paper, answer the questions that follow.*

"ROLL ON, COLUMBIA"
by Woody Guthrie
Roll on, Columbia, roll on.
Roll on, Columbia, roll on.
Your power is turning our darkness to
   dawn,
So roll on, Columbia, roll on!

Green Douglas firs where the waters cut
   through.
Down her wild mountains and canyons
   she flew.
Canadian Northwest to the oceans so blue,
Roll on, Columbia, roll on!

Other great rivers add power to you,
Yakima, Snake, and the Klickitat too,
Sandy Willamette and Hood River too,
Roll on, Columbia, roll on.

Tom Jefferson's vision would not let him
   rest,
An empire he saw in the Pacific Northwest.
Sent Lewis and Clark and they did the rest,
Roll on, Columbia, roll on.

Source: Available online at http://www.netstate.com/states/
symb/song/wa_roll_on_columbia.htm.

It's there on your banks that we fought
   many a fight,
Sheridan's boys in the blockhouse that
   night,
They saw us in death but never in flight,
Roll on, Columbia, roll on.

At Bonneville now there are ships in the
   locks,
The waters have risen and cleared all the
   rocks,
Shiploads of plenty will steam past the
   docks,
So roll on, Columbia, roll on.

And on up the river is Grand Coulee Dam,
The mightiest thing ever built by a man,
To run the great factories and water the
   land,
It's roll on, Columbia, roll on.

These mighty men labored by day and by
   night,
Matching their strength 'gainst the river's
   wild flight,
Through rapids and falls, they won the
   hard fight,
Roll on, Columbia, roll on.

Questions to Think About

1. What is the purpose of this folk song?

2. List two descriptive phrases Guthrie used to describe the river.

3. **Draw Inferences** In reading the lyrics, what do you think the working conditions

were like for those who worked on building the dam?

4. **Draw Conclusions** How did the building of the dam change the lives of those living in rural areas in the Pacific Northwest?

THE NEW DEAL

Section 1 Quiz

A. Key Terms and People

Directions: *From Column II below, choose the term or person that best fits each description. You will not use all of the answers.*

Column I

_____ 1. became the President's "eyes and ears" during the first New Deal

_____ 2. priest who criticized the New Deal

_____ 3. signed into law fifteen pieces of legislation in the first hundred days of office

_____ 4. introduced a "Share Our Wealth" program

_____ 5. program to insure bank deposits

_____ 6. built a series of dams to generate electric power

Column II

a. Charles Coughlin

b. Franklin D. Roosevelt

c. Eleanor Roosevelt

d. Huey Long

e. fireside chat

f. FDIC

g. TVA

h. NRA

B. Key Concepts

Directions: *Write the letter of the best answer or ending in the blank.*

_____ 7. What were the goals of the New Deal?

    a. reform the government and decrease spending

    b. create schools and protect farmers

    c. increase spending on defense and trade

    d. provide relief, recovery, and reform

_____ 8. Some opponents of the New Deal believed that it

    a. benefited only the banking industry.

    b. harmed home owners.

    c. threatened individual freedom.

    d. gave too much power to the people.

_____ 9. The American Liberty League formed to

    a. support the Bonus Army.

    b. introduce new legislation.

    c. oppose FDR's New Deal.

    d. oppose the TVA

_____ 10. The Agricultural Adjustment Act helped farmers because it

    a. sought to end overproduction and raise crop prices.

    b. attracted industry with the promise of cheap power.

    c. created jobs for over 2 million U.S. citizens.

    d. regulated the stock market and made investments safer.

THE NEW DEAL

Section 2 Quiz

A. Reviewing Key Terms and People

Directions: *Circle the term or person in parentheses that best completes the sentence.*

1. The (CIO/WPA) helped build and improve the nation's highways.

2. Putting money in the hands of consumers so that they can buy more goods in order to stimulate the economy is called (pump priming/collective bargaining).

3. In 1938, the (Wagner Act/Fair Labor Standards Act) established a minimum wage and a maximum workweek of 44 hours.

4. President Roosevelt was accused of (court packing/a sit-down strike) when he attempted to increase the number of Justices on the Supreme Court.

5. (Owen J. Roberts/John Maynard Keynes) was a British economist who believed that deficit spending was necessary to provide the necessary relief from the depression.

6. President Roosevelt introduced the (Second New Deal/Social Security Act) to help retirees.

B. Key Concepts

Directions: *Write the letter of the best answer or ending in the blank.*

_____ 7. The Rural Electrification Administration provided electricity to

    a. the elderly.   **c.** the unemployed.

    b. farmers.   **d.** minorities.

_____ 8. The right to collective bargaining was part of the

    a. Wagner Act.   **c.** Social Security Act.

    b. Works Progress Administration.   **d.** Agricultural Adjustment Act.

_____ 9. Members of the _____ participated in a sit down strike until General Motors agreed to recognize them.

    a. WPA   **c.** REA

    b. UAW   **d.** NLRB

_____ 10. What caused Republicans to gain power in Congress in 1938?

    a. The Supreme Court started approving New Deal programs.

    b. The economy took a downturn and wiped out much of FDR's progress.

    c. Unemployment went down from 14 percent to 10 percent.

    d. Southern Democrats became supporters of the New Deal.

THE NEW DEAL
Section 3 Quiz

A. Key Terms and People

Directions: *Read the following statements. If a statement is correct, write T next to the sentence. If a statement is incorrect, write F next to the sentence and replace the underlined word(s) to make the statement correct.*

_____ 1. The <u>Indian New Deal</u> provided funding for the construction of new schools and hospitals.

_____ 2. The President had a group of African American advisors that became known as the <u>New Deal coalition</u>.

_____ 3. FDR named <u>Mary McLeod Bethune</u> the Commissioner of Indian Affairs.

_____ 4. Roosevelt's programs led to the rise of a <u>welfare state</u> in the United States.

_____ 5. The <u>Dawes Act</u> brought together southern whites, northern blue collar workers, poor Midwestern farmers, and African Americans.

B. Key Concepts

Directions: *Write the letter of the best answer or ending in the blank.*

_____ 6. Eleanor Roosevelt showed her support of minorities when she
   a. appointed herself as Secretary of Labor.
   b. sat with black delegates at a conference.
   c. wrote a weekly newspaper column.
   d. established a minimum wage.

_____ 7. During the 1930s, the Bureau of Indian Affairs
   a. passed acts that led to total landlessness.
   b. denied Native Americans the right to vote.
   c. stopped discouraging the practice of Indian religions.
   d. encouraged Native Americans to herd sheep on the Colorado Plateau.

_____ 8. FDR set aside 12 million acres of land for
   a. Indian reservations.   c. dams.
   b. farms.   d. national parks.

_____ 9. How many terms did Roosevelt serve as President?
   a. 1   c. 2
   b. 3   d. 4

_____ 10. Who was the first female Cabinet member?
   a. Frances Perkins   c. Mary McLeod Bethune
   b. Margaret Marshall   d. Eleanor Roosevelt

THE NEW DEAL

Section 4 Quiz

A. Key Terms and People

Directions: *Complete each sentence with the correct term or person. You will not use all of the answers.*

Frank Capra	murals	John Steinbeck	Ginger Rogers
War of the Worlds	*The Wizard of Oz*	Lillian Hellman	Glenn Miller

1. Artists painted large pictures called _____ on public buildings to celebrate the people who helped build the nation.

2. _____ is one of the most memorable Depression-era movies because it showed people that their dreams could come true.

3. Director _____ made movies that showed the strength of average Americans.

4. _____ wrote a novel about the Joad family.

5. 1930s playwright _____ wrote socially conscious plays featuring strong female roles.

6. _____ was a radio program that caused panic.

B. Key Concepts

Directions: *Write the letter of the best answer or ending in the blank.*

_____ 7. Who was a top swing musician?
- a. Glenn Miller
- b. Orson Welles
- c. Woody Guthrie
- d. Billie Holiday

_____ 8. One way that Americans escaped their concerns during the 1930s was to
- a. live in the country.
- b. follow the stock market.
- c. go to theaters to watch movies.
- d. avoid watching news on television.

_____ 9. *The Lone Ranger* and *The Shadow* are examples of
- a. big bands.
- b. Depression-era novels.
- c. Broadway musicals.
- d. radio series.

_____ 10. The Federal Art Project set a precedent for
- a. increased government support of radicals.
- b. federal funding of the arts and artists.
- c. free theater performances for the public.
- d. realistically showing living conditions on farms.

THE NEW DEAL

Test A

A. Key Terms and People

Directions: *From Column II below, choose the person or term that correctly completes each description. You will not use all of the answers. (3 points each)*

Column I

_____ 1. Louisiana Senator _____ introduced the "Share Our Wealth" program.

_____ 2. Putting money in consumers' hands so they can buy goods and stimulate the economy is called _____.

_____ 3. _____ advised the president and championed racial equality.

_____ 4. A government that is responsible for the welfare of certain citizens is a _____.

_____ 5. United Auto Workers staged a 44-day _____ against General Motors.

_____ 6. When FDR tried to put more judges on the Supreme Court, his action was called _____.

_____ 7. The _____ paid artists to paint large murals.

_____ 8. The _____ built and improved highways, dredged rivers, and promoted conservation.

_____ 9. _____ wrote the novel *The Grapes of Wrath* about the Joad family.

_____ 10. Unions used _____ to achieve goals.

Column II

a. Mary McLeod Bethune

b. Federal Art Project

c. sit-down strike

d. court packing

e. John Steinbeck

f. pump priming

g. welfare state

h. Works Progress Administration

i. Huey Long

j. collective bargaining

B. Key Concepts

Directions: *Write the letter of the best answer or ending in the blank. (3 points each)*

_____ 11. To deal with the banking crisis, FDR and Congress passed the

a. Federal Deposit Insurance Corporation.

b. Emergency Banking Bill.

c. Bonus Army Act.

_____ **12.** What did the FDIC insure?
  a. bank deposits
  b. farm loans
  c. business investments

Directions: *Use the following quotation to answer question 13.*

> Sec. 7. Employees shall have the right to self-organization, to form, join, or assist labor organizations, to bargain collectively through representatives of their own choosing . . .
>
> —*National Labor Relations Act, 1935*

_____ **13.** The National Labor Relations Act gave workers the right to
  a. set a minimum wage.
  b. develop industries codes.
  c. join labor unions.

_____ **14.** The Indian Reorganization Act of 1934 prevented
  a. Indians from receiving Social Security.
  b. further Indian land divisions.
  c. soil erosion.

_____ **15.** The _____ brought together southern whites, northern blue collar workers, poor Midwestern farmers, and African Americans to form a strong political force.
  a. Dawes Act
  b. Black Cabinet
  c. New Deal Coalition

_____ **16.** The _____ provided jobs for men, replanted forests, and fought fires.
  a. Civilian Conservation Corps
  b. Federal Emergency Relief Act
  c. Tennessee Valley Authority

_____ **17.** What were the main goals of the Tennessee Valley Authority?
  a. jobs and subsidies
  b. flood control and electricity
  c. insurance and health care

_____ **18.** Eleanor Roosevelt showed her deep political involvement in government when she
  a. won approval for the Fair Labor Standards Act.
  b. ended gender discrimination in the workplace.
  c. offered FDR advice on policy issues.

_____ **19.** How did New Deal programs change life in the West?
  a. introduced labor unions and minimum wage
  b. built dams to supply power and to stop flooding
  c. cut taxes and encouraged farmers to stop grazing sheep

_____ **20.** What were the two main forms of entertainment during the depression era?
  a. radio and movies
  b. television and murals
  c. newspapers and theater

Name _____ Class _____ Date _____

C. Document-Based Assessment

Directions: *Use the political cartoon to answer questions 21 and 22 on the back of this paper or on a separate sheet of paper. (10 points)*

New Deal ties up government resources, The Conde Nast Publications, Inc.

21. Interpret Visuals What are the ties holding down the United States?

D. Critical Thinking

Directions: *Answer the questions below on the back of this paper or on a separate sheet of paper. (15 points each)*

22. Contrast What were some of the criticisms of President Roosevelt and his New Deal programs? Choose two criticisms and explain them.

23. Draw Conclusions How did New Deal programs help American farmers? How did New Deal programs hurt American farmers? Overall, did the New Deal help or hurt American farmers?

Test B

A. Key Terms and People

Directions: *From Column II below, choose the person or term that best fits each description. You will not use all of the answers. (3 points each)*

Column I

_____ 1. Louisiana Senator who opposed the New Deal

_____ 2. putting money in consumers' hands to stimulate the economy

_____ 3. member of the Black Cabinet

_____ 4. formed when the government assumes responsibility for providing for citizens' needs

_____ 5. protest used against General Motors

_____ 6. name for FDR's attempt to change the Supreme Court

_____ 7. New Deal program that funded large murals

_____ 8. New Deal program created to build and improve highways

_____ 9. writer of *The Grapes of Wrath*

_____ 10. allowed union members to negotiate about hours and wages

Column II

a. Mary McLeod Bethune

b. Federal Art Project

c. sit-down strike

d. court packing

e. John Steinbeck

f. pump priming

g. welfare state

h. WPA

i. Huey Long

j. fireside chats

k. collective bargaining

l. social security

B. Key Concepts

Directions: *Write the letter of the best answer or ending in the blank. (3 points each)*

_____ 11. What did Roosevelt and Congress pass the day after FDR's inauguration?
   a. Federal Art Project   c. Federal Emergency Relief Act
   b. Emergency Banking Bill   d. Agricultural Adjustment Act

_____ 12. Roosevelt created the Securities Exchange Commission to
   a. regulate the stock market.
   b. ensure bank deposits.
   c. give banks a chance to organize.
   d. pay farmers to destroy their livestock.

Name _____ Class _____ Date _____

Directions: *Use the following quotation to answer question 13.*

> "Experience has proved that protection by law of the right of employees to organize and bargain collectively safeguards commerce from injury, impairment, or interruption, and promotes the flow of commerce . . . by restoring equality of bargaining power between employers and employees."
>
> —*National Labor Relations Act, 1935*

_____ 13. What reason does the National Labor Relations Act give for allowing labor unions to form?

    a. Labor unions make conditions safer in workplaces.

    b. The flow of commerce cannot continue without collective bargaining.

    c. Collective bargaining ensures equality and protects the flow of business.

    d. Experience proves that workers are interrupted if collective bargaining exists.

_____ 14. The Indian Reorganization Act of 1934 prohibited

    a. Native Americans from receiving Social Security.

    b. government from further dividing Native American land.

    c. tribes from governing their lands.

    d. people from grazing their sheep.

_____ 15. The New Deal Coalition was a strong political force that

    a. encouraged African Americans to vote for Republicans.

    b. prevented Native Americans from voting in elections.

    c. gave Democrats a majority in both houses of Congress for many years.

    d. brought wealthy people more power in the federal government.

_____ 16. Which of the following extended job opportunities to Mexican Americans and other minority youth?

    a. Civilian Conservation Corps   **c.** Tennessee Valley Authority

    b. Federal Emergency Relief Act   **d.** Federal Writers' Project

_____ 17. Critics disapproved of the Tennessee Valley Authority because it

    a. distributed money to people outside the Tennessee Valley.

    b. gave government direct control of a business.

    c. paid farmers to kill off excess livestock.

    d. built dams to control flood waters.

_____ 18. How did Eleanor Roosevelt change the role of the First Lady?

    a. The role became an elected position with Congressional voting rights.

    b. She created a newspaper column that all First Ladies now have to write.

    c. The role changed from being largely ceremonial to a role of political involvement.

    d. She created a new Cabinet position for herself that all First Ladies since have held.

_____ **19.** The Bonneville Dam and other similar projects improved

    a. irrigation in California.   **c.** tenant farming.

    b. life in the American West.   **d.** travel in the Midwest.

_____ **20.** People turned to radio and movies in the 1930s to

    a. escape their troubles.   **c.** listen for ways to save money.

    b. celebrate industrial workers.   **d.** learn more about the depression.

C. Document-Based Assessment

Directions: *Use the political cartoon to answer questions 21 and 22 on the back of this paper or on a separate sheet of paper. (10 points)*

New Deal ties up government resources, The Conde Nast Publications, Inc.

21. Interpret Visuals What are the ties holding down the United States?

D. Critical Thinking

Directions: *Answer the question below on the back of this paper or on a separate sheet of paper. (15 points each)*

22. Contrast President Roosevelt's New Deal was criticized for doing too much and doing too little. Choose two critics from each side and contrast their arguments.

23. Draw Conclusions How did New Deal programs both help and hurt American farmers? How effective was the New Deal in aiding American farmers?

Answer Key

Vocabulary Builder

Students' answers should demonstrate understanding of the vocabulary.

Reading Strategy

1. People criticized the New Deal for many different reasons.
2. Possible answers: Many conservatives thought that the New Deal was making the government too big and powerful. Some socialists and populists thought that the New Deal needed to do more to help people.
3. Possible question: How did other people feel about FDR's opponents, Charles Coughlin and Huey Long?

Enrichment

Students' projects should demonstrate research, creative thinking, and appropriate presentation. Use *Assessment Rubrics* to evaluate the project.

Issues Connector

1. The timeline indicates that the government has a history of involving itself in the economy, with a large involvement between 1890 and 1933.
2. The Sherman Antitrust Act allows anyone who is hurt in their person or their business by trust activities the right to sue the company or person.
3. He would probably think the act was important, because he believes businesses instead of farmers are becoming wealthy.
4. Bush argues that the American people can spend their money more effectively than the government can, and the American people have made the economy better.

5. FDR probably would have said that this Act was necessary for the general welfare of the country. He might also say that he was regulating commerce between the states because food grown in one state may be shipped to other states.
6. Students may say that they would vote for a President who promotes government control of the economy because then businesses would not be able to harm consumers, or other businesses, and people would be protected. Other students may say that they would vote for a President who opposes government control of the economy because then they would pay less money in taxes.

Interpreting Political Cartoons
The New Deal

1. The bottles represent the New Deal "remedies" that are being used to cure the "sickness" of the Great Depression.
2. Congress, represented by a nurse, appears happy to support FDR with the New Deal programs.
3. Possible answers: Yes, because Congress and Uncle Sam, representing the country, appear to be happy about FDR's remedies. No, because FDR seems to be giving many medicines to Uncle Sam and telling the nurse (Congress) that they may not work, which makes FDR appear uncertain.

FDR and the New Deal

1. He is leading the country and Congress toward his new legislation.
2. Possible answer: The cartoon shows FDR single-handedly pulling the Congress to action. FDR seems to be in charge of Congress.
3. The cartoonist probably thinks that FDR is leading the people in the right direction; he is smiling and confident.

Answer Key

Reading a Chart

1. Many of the programs were referred to by their initials (WPA, FDIC), or just a mix of letters like alphabet soup.
2. The WPA, CCC, and NYA created jobs for the unemployed.
3. Possible answer: The government spent billions of dollars to create many programs run by the federal government.
4. FDR probably believed that it was the government's job to help people during the depression.

Biography

1. women's rights, minority rights, and helping the poor
2. She helped refugees from World War II enter the United States.
3. The typical First Lady did not actively pursue legislation or push her own agendas; Eleanor Roosevelt probably had to come up against the beliefs of her husband at times.
4. She might be grateful that Eleanor Roosevelt changed the role of First Lady allowing the present First Lady to address her own concerns.

Link to Literature

1. to honor the Columbia River and its place in the building of the Northwest
2. Possible answers: Green Douglas firs where the waters cut through; At Bonneville now there are ships in the locks; river's wild flight; rapids and falls
3. The song says that the people worked day and night, so they must have worked long hours. It also says that they worked against "the river's wild flight, through rapids and falls," which indicates that it was difficult terrain and hard work.
4. The people no longer had to rely on fire and candles for heat and light. With electric power, their lives were made easier.

Section 1 Quiz

1. c   2. a   3. b   4. d   5. f
6. g   7. d   8. c   9. c   10. a

Section 2 Quiz

1. WPA
2. pump priming
3. Fair Labor Standards Act
4. court packing
5. John Maynard Keynes
6. Social Security Act
7. b   8. a   9. b   10. b

Section 3 Quiz

1. T
2. F, Black Cabinet
3. F, John Collier
4. T
5. F, New Deal coalition
6. b   7. c   8. d   9. d   10. a

Section 4 Quiz

1. murals
2. *The Wizard of Oz*
3. Frank Capra
4. John Steinbeck
5. Lillian Hellman
6. *War of the Worlds*
7. a   8. c   9. d   10. b

Test A

1. i   2. f   3. a   4. g   5. c
6. d   7. b   8. h   9. e   10. j
11. b   12. a   13. c   14. b   15. c
16. a   17. b   18. c   19. b   20. a
21. The ties holding down the United States are the New Deal programs.

Answer Key

22. Possible answer: Some people thought that the programs gave the government too much power and took away individual freedoms. Critics formed the American Liberty League. Some Supreme Court justices also thought that Roosevelt was overstepping his powers as President and ruled many of his programs unconstitutional. Some people believed that Roosevelt was creating an imperial presidency because of the amount of power he held. Others thought that the programs did not do enough. Communists and socialists claimed that the new programs benefited only the wealthy. Francis Townsend, Charles Coughlin, and Huey Long argued that more should be done to help poor Americans and offered plans for giving direct aid to Americans from the federal government.

23. Possible answer: Farmers benefited from subsidies and programs designed to bring electricity to rural areas. Farmers also benefited from dams, irrigation systems, sewage systems, and hydroelectric plants that were built by New Deal programs. Sharecroppers and tenant farmers often did not benefit from New Deal programs designed to help farmers. Others said that New Deal programs benefited larger farms more than smaller farms. Overall, New Deal programs benefited farmers because crop prices and land prices rose, more farmers had electricity, and flooding and sewage control benefited many people.

Test B

1. i	2. f	3. a	4. g	5. c
6. d	7. b	8. h	9. e	10. k
11. b	12. a	13. c	14. b	15. c
16. a	17. b	18. c	19. b	20. a

21. The ties holding down the United States are the New Deal programs.

22. Possible answer: Some people thought that the programs gave the government too much power. President Herbert Hoover criticized the New Deal, and President Taft agreed that the New Deal threatened individual freedom. Some Supreme Court justices also thought that Roosevelt was overstepping his powers as President and ruled many of his programs unconstitutional. Others thought that the programs did not do enough. Communists and socialists claimed that the new programs benefited only the wealthy. Francis Townsend, Charles Coughlin, and Huey Long argued that more should be done to help poor Americans and offered plans for giving direct aid to Americans from the federal government.

23. Possible answer: Farmers benefited from subsidies and programs designed to bring electricity to rural areas. Farmers also benefited from dams, irrigation systems, sewage systems, and hydroelectric plants that were built by New Deal programs. Sharecroppers and tenant farmers often did not benefit from New Deal programs designed to help farmers. Others said that New Deal programs benefited larger farms more than smaller farms. Overall, New Deal programs were effective in aiding farmers because crop prices and land prices rose, more farmers had electricity, and flooding and sewage control benefited many people.

CURRICULUM